T0041306

A Case of Love and Hate:
The Book of Quotes
*
Volume 1

Chenjerai Mhondera

Mwanaka Media and Publishing Pvt Ltd,
Chitungwiza Zimbabwe

*

Creativity, Wisdom and Beauty

Publisher:
Mmap

Mwanaka Media and Publishing Pvt Ltd

24 Svosve Road, Zengeza 1

Chitungwiza Zimbabwe

mwanaka@yahoo.com

https//mwanakamediaandpublishing.weebly.com

Distributed in and outside N. America by African Books Collective

orders@africanbookscollective.com

www.africanbookscollective.com

ISBN: 978-0-7974-8494-8

EAN: 9780797484948

© Chenjerai Mhondera 2018

All rights reserved.

No part of this book may be reproduced or transmitted in any form or by any means, mechanical or electronic, including photocopying and recording, or be stored in any information storage or retrieval system, without written permission from the publisher

DISCLAIMER

All views expressed in this publication are those of the author and do not necessarily reflect the views of *Mmap*.

Acknowledgements

I would like to thank the people of Zimbabwe; from the ordinary citizens in streets, peasants in countrysides, civil servants in public offices, students in schools and universities, ordinary poor man starving, rich people, the politicians of the day, religious groups, security structures of the land right up to the topmost authority of the land. I thank you, Zimbabweans sincerely for being a practical example for my case study. I cannot avoid mentioning the SADC region and it's leaders as well as the entire people of Africa. You helped whether consciously or unconsciously to make this project a success. In my humblest state, I cannot avoid mentioning my Editor Tendai R Mwanaka for regrouping these quotes into specific themes and smaller volumes as the book is in this sizeable form. I want to admit that the book was big, with over 6 900 quotes altogether, but despite how mixed up and ardous the task was to select the quotes, Mwanaka sacrificed his time and committed his energy to such an uneasy task. It is such a sacrifice that cannot go unmentioned. To my family and friends, I say thank you for your love and support. To Cathrine Sithole, I say thank you for your companionship and life support. To COMRADE Innocent Mil, I have not forgotten those times I was a hermit in Zimbabwe when you visited me and sacrificed your time to be with me at my place and at campsites; as we had those healthy discussions and reflections about the situation in Zimbabwe and Africa. I surely haven't forgotten when you reinforced my idea to come up with a book of quotes. The practical support, criticism, reflections, reviews and approval you volunteered to give as I read my quotes to you about everything in that voluminous book. You were a reliable COMRADE during those moments of my hermit. I salute you. My publisher, Mwanaka Media and Publishing Pvt Ltd, receive my heartfelt gratitude.

_____

Introduction

The world as it stands is in crises due to serious political blunders maybe regarded as micro issues background in whatever circle. The economy of the World is crumbling and the social crust on which we are grounded is seriously shaking and breaking apiece and apart under political negligence of some leaders in this universe. Zimbabwe of Africa, as well as Africa of the World cannot be spared in this political sequence. So herein the collection of political quotes, formed and created by Cecil Jones Myondela (Chenjerai Mhondera) are a set of what the World cannot ignore if they want real heritage and wisdom about insights, visions, aims and objectives of what governments of Africa seek to achieve and what the people of such governments seek to have in order to realize their dreams of a fully liberated African society with respect for human rights and liberties. And Africa's interdependence and development, competitiveness and excellence on global politics, and as well as flourishing on global economic market in line with millennium goals of peace, unity, democracy, hard work, and the likes. The quotes in this book are based on practical realities of the ordeals the author captured, suffered, experienced under the Government of Mugabe during his course of research and survey in Zimbabwe. Henceforth the book of Great Quotes which will be in series is history past, history present, and history future as it describes practical experiences of the past, captures realities of now and predicts or forecast the future. In this book Mugabe seems immortalised as Zimbabwe and Africa themselves as he is described in and out with no fear or favour- the objective being to give a clearer picture and view of the World round us from an insider report. Mugabe is in some cases regarded as the Democracy of Africa while others regard him as the principal dictator of the entire world, an enigma of authoritarian or tyrant rule in Zimbabwe and a shameless and ruthless defendant of Marxist ideology or philosophy in Africa. The Case of Love and Hate unfolds in this book in a way that will leave the World not bankrupt of literature regarding this enigma of our history.

Can Africa remain a victim in the hands of extremism and a colony in the hands of minority rule; whether black minority rule or white minority rule? Surely not! Africa need to be freed from such paws of ignorance and negligence, jaws of oppression and extremism, and from laws that infringe the Democratic rights and liberties of a people of this society.

Nonetheless this seeming elementary particularity on Mugabe, Zimbabwe and Africa does not suggest that the quotes exclude other societies outside Africa. No! They are included since Africa like other societies in the globe, is not an island. It survives as it links and creates meaningful webs and connections with the world outside it. The attitude and reaction of other continents is still by and large a source of concern if Africa indeed is to emerge as a super power or giant on the political chessboard, economic chart and social map of the globe. The forces of dynamism and modernism cannot be ignored in this power play as Africa reflexes and flexes its muscles.

The book which comes in volumes has no preceding volume. It is original in this first volume, which will be followed by subsequent volumes already preserved and reserved in our files of important literature as we speak. Do not miss your chance to read from this book, if ever you intend to be a leader and enhance yourself in this philosophy of politics, as you stand a chance to become sound in your political stature and career and be able to improve the people you lead or intend to lead in your society.

Politics is not only a game of politicians as the generality of our people might need to associate it with Presidents and their cabinet as well as the government's security structures. Politics is administration and wherever administration exists, politics is involved. In religion (churches, synagogues, temples etc), in economy (ndustries and factories etc) and in education (schools, colleges and universities) and as well as in family setups- politics exists. Henceforth it is imperative for whosoever, anywhere, intending to asume leadership or already a leader to consider seriously reading this book published under specific themes and in different volumes.

QUOTES

The world is revolving around dead mentalities- and it will take a whole revolution, to have this world wake up and, embrace a paradigm shift and start to work to its normal mode

******

Do not allow the politics of your country or society to rot the talent in you. If you do allow it, you will never be a genius in this world.

******

Global input is my doctrine of life. If it was injected into me, then I would call it a syring of right dosage... it is the world that matters to me... Zimbabwe is too small to contain me... I need hundreds of countries like Zimbabwe to circumcise me into abandoning my dream of the world.

****

I am not proudly Zimbabwean, neither am I proudly African nor proudly whatever because Zimbabwe is in me, Africa is in me and the world wholly is proudly in me.

******

I know it's hard to kill a whole generation with fear. The case in point is of Peter refusing to accept that Jesus Christ is his lord when Peter was to face death like his master. And the majority sellouts and volunteers who vowed to remain behind when the guerillas sacrificed to liberate a society from the white minority rule. It is only when we know that to live long in a society where majority rule means suffrage of majority is to spell politics and wealth of a society in the hands of so few, and to live less of a citizen. I don't desire to live long in a society with no respect for citizenry. What's liberty or independence if the wealth and health of the society continues to be in the hands of the minority? Whether minority White or minority Black, minority Pink or minority Yellow- minority is minority, period! All those are colour blind racism. I have always said, I don't fear to die, to disappear or to be assassinated for what I believe is right and good for us all. While being disappeared or assassinated has been treated with common fears or phobia and avoided by many, I personally see or perceive and understand it as a heroic send off of a legendary or a veteran. I feel great to die by the bite of a bayonet or a revolver than to die from a mosquito bite, HIV and AIDS or a starving, poor, jobless citizen.

******

Excellence and diplomacy are two stubborn words. While diplomacy is an ability to deal with challenges without making your neighbour suspect you of foul play, excellence is an ability to rule in the face of threatening failure or challenge an existing rivalry. In life we struggle to combine or harmonize these two, and whoever is able to combine them, indeed is an achiever. Excellency is when your weaknesses are compared against your strengths and still you sustain to emerge an achiever. Excellency is not when you are compared to against individuals or cooperatives and distinguished a winner.

******

Good governance is when our promise to the people does not become their grievances against us any time in the future. I want the message to be clear to a politician that a promise if it doesn't materialize is a failure in future.

******

In a society where my father is a tyrant, I am a prince with no liberty. My father doesn't have to breach principles of Democracy and Human rights for him to become a tyrant. He has to make me not free after speech.

******

To teach a culture of peace in a society is to do or give the citizen little if it is all the best a politician has. Don't bully citizen, disappear them and spell a wave of fear unless the politician shall remain the supreme law himself.

******

I always think to rule is no to ruin.

******

Every society is a colony, but what differs is that some societies are not as extreme as the rule of the tyrant. In some societies, it is constructive to criticise a government if praise fail to better and benefit a society whereas in some societies it is treasonous and dangerous to criticise a government if it fails to deliver.

******

Have you ever heard of Mugabe as a legend? And as an ardent follower of him shall I be condemned and persecuted for believing that Mugabe is a religion?

******

When you are a colony in mind, you always think you are not free everywhere you are.

******

When you expect to live large and in luxury at the expense of the majority, you are indeed a sellout.

******

If it be true that man is born free but everywhere he is in chains, then be a free bandit, rather than a prisoner.

******

People are not like a penis. Together we stand, divided we fall. The only thing I know to rise and stand even without company is a penis at the pulse of ejaculation.

******

Desire to be freed, if it's not your determination to free yourself, it is like a door which even when slam shut violently against its own frame, it continues to lock with all easy and without making an effort to part from hinges. Similarly it is like a Christian slave applying the principle of forgiving to his

unrepentant devil master while they (Christian slave) continues to
suffer under the oppressive rule.

******

When the slave is a forgiving sufferer, then when a
liberator comes the liberator shall see no difference between
simplicity and stupidity, sacrifice and suffering.

******

The first person to create a happening or activity was an
ARTIST, but the first person to kill or destroy a happening was a
POLITICIAN. That's why a Politician and an Artist are never
friends.

******

We are very clear on what Africa should do as an
independent society. Our joy of being liberated should not be
confused or compromised all the same simply because we are
foreigners elsewhere.

******

My people and I are neither a renegade nor a rebel.
Together we are a society, alone one is a rebel.

******

When you say politics is a dirty game what do you mean when the President is the smartest person in every society?

******

We shall be a Government later. For now we are just, but a social grouping.

******

If I don't write a book about Mugabe, I shall keep speaking a book about Mugabe.

******

When we talk of trails of rampant destruction by politicians, we get the stigma of being accused of having become oppositional movements or aligning to factions. Are we a fraction anyway to be accused of being not a whole number in politics?

******

A Tyrant is not a politician who put people in jail in order to maintain law and order. A Tyrant is a politician who kills the economic fate of a people and their livelihood and threaten to kill, jail, or disappear them when they rise against him.

******

We are not demanding too much from a corrupt politician. We demand that you vacate office, dissolve all properties and surrender what you stole from the people and owe to the Government as soon as you read this. Don't delay or try to resist, because we are marching to your doorstep. If you don't hear the knock on the door, it shall be you knocked down!

******

In a Free State, people in jail are offenders. They are either criminals or captives of war. They can't be neither nor! Our jails do not belong to those of Free States. Ours are shut-up camps for free citizens and acute critics of the Government.

******

In this society you are either a prisoner or free elsewhere. If you are free, join the demonstrators and strikers to have prisoners liberated, freed, or released.

******

After putting so much trust to vote and give you the power to protect our rights and liberty, has the onus on you become that of killing, disappearing and throwing us in jail? Oh Mr. Politician sir, you are an ungrateful idiot!

******

Why do I have to reserve respect for a Cabinet that bullies my society? How long shall fear ruin my people to salute their Conquerors as if they are their liberators?

******

I do respect Americans and Europeans in their own rights and respects as Sovereign Societies, independent of foreign politics and policies. I wish them to translate the same respect, not fear for their mightiness, but to reciprocate that to Africa or any other society for a sustainable interdependent relationship to exist amongst us as a global village, together with the silent and amicable Asian and Australian communities.

******

What we have in Zimbabwe as economic blue-print is not ZIM-ASSET, but a ZIM-FUTSEKI. It is rather an insult to our socio-economic structure and emancipation. The intention is good, but the implementation is poor.

******

To expect Government attention and back-up to come so easily on art or writings, that even bite such Governments, is just but the pulse of an idiot. Writers are no friends of State. Period! They are pawns in the political chess game. We force Politicians and Governments to accept our rule. So every artist everywhere there it is your task to take responsibility to have art and writings that impact on the lives of everyone, Government included.

******

A government with no capacity to buy her citizens caskets and accord them a descent burial will never depart from her habit of sending her citizens missing.

******

I have never followed the rot of my father because my brother behind me pulled me back, and I feared I might fall by the backside.

******

One of the worst struggles is that which we have not yet fought. It is being fought silently, and when the conflict is out, all the rest shall join war and real shooting shall start.

******

I believe politicians are creators of war elsewhere. They deprive citizens of their wealth and rights. Did I say they deny them freedom? Oh yes they take the mass for granted, and lie about citizens' welfare, wealth, and freedom- and keep oppressing them (citizens) in their silence.

******

For how long shall we be foreigners in a world of liberties? Shall we continue to wallow in poverty, and to be swallowed and intimidated by their revolvers?

******

One reason why you are not free is because your freedom is as prisoner tied to an individual somewhere. Find the culprit, and free your freedom. Do not demand your freedom, it won't be given to you- just free it!

******

So many a time politicians think they are no offenders of peace in their own societies. Am I corrupt to write that politicians are corrupt? So did I cause war? But politicians lie that artists cause war. We sing war they cause! We write war they cause!

******

Do I seem to support war? Oh no, I support peace! But if peace comes as terms upon me I refuse. I support peace as a matter of choice- not as a directive from my oppressors!

******

Wherever freedom of mankind is a topic,, I do talk about the freedom of my neighbour because my freedom is the right and duty of my neighbour to safeguard against oppressors. What do I mean? Together we are freed.

******

A false comrade is a persecutor of his countrymen.

******

I seem to be inspired by a world of radicals, extremists...
While it might be true that their world is short-lived, they are time
definers and break webs of lies created by hypocrites.

******

Politics is colour without identity. No matter how
politicians paint it with numerous colours, it remains a colour
mystery.

******

A commoner is a colour of persecutions. It is up to
a commoner to resist or continue to be haunted by the gods of
persecution.

******

Father, forgive Africa a rich beggar for the idiocy of her
Presidents cursed by gods of education, religion and seeming
civilization of the West. Shall I say Africans are being consumed in
the plagues of this curse? Oh yes, forgive them Father!

******

If you are a politician do not kill the civilians in your
society because when those who want development rise to power,

they will not have enough manpower to help them develop the society.

******

Unless I become a rebel, this society shall never, never know what it means to be independent!

******

The destiny of this society was stolen by selfishness and greediness of some corrupt individuals. Identify these culprits and recover her destiny.

******

Do not discourage or stigmatize those who want to distinguish themselves as politicians because everybody, one way or the other is a politician. Period! The only difference is that, the majority of us are hypocrites, cowards and sellouts.

******

The worst and dangerous politician is a civilian. Do not take them for granted or mistake their identity as a colour of no harm!

******

When a government wants to exist no more, it becomes an island away from its people and ceases to address their grievances.

******

When a government nears its death, it first persecutes its citizens before getting buried by the citizens.

******

No man is an island. Even the Presidents have ears elsewhere.

******

A President is the only prisoner who goes without being handcuffed, but everywhere they go they are escorted like prisoners.

******

In Zimbabwe, the business people are more learned than the general educated cursed lot of civilians. If the civilians don't strike and demonstrate against BOND NOTES, the Business-people will strike and demonstrate against CIVILIANS, by hoarding or withdrawing their commodities from the market. And who shall suffer and die? The CIVILIANS, of course!

******

The deeds of this corrupt Regime are written on the Bearer's Cheque of 2008. If you think Bond Notes will bring any wonder, just watch and wait to perish in hunger and food shortages, inflation and abnormal price increases!

******

If patience pays- in Zimbabwe, POLITICIANS could have understood that BOND NOTES are not a means to pay the Civilians or Civil servants.

******

When I said I am writing about the true deeds of this corrupt regime, someone scared me that the CIO will disappear you! I replied, 'Disappear me? Disappear me for what? Nonsense, I am not writing about politics or lying about anything or even politicking here! I am writing and speaking about the welfare of citizens, the CIO included. This Bond Notes or bond money is NONSENSE. Period! And when this Bond thing comes, it will not affect the Civilians only. It will affect the Soldiers, Police Officers, CID and CIO, and everyone else. We know that from

2008- and do you think the CIO, as you scare me, are part and parcel of this NONSENSE? When hunger and food shortages come, they will not spare the CIO! Inflation and price increase will affect everyone else! And so what's the nonsense you tell me? Am I talking about politics, the rallies and campaigns of whoever and whichever Party? Of course, not! We are talking about the truth of our being- our welfare particularly, as citizens of this society. This nonsense fucks up your head. Scared, scared of what? I am not talking about politics here! If I am, then I am talking about the politics of the stomach! If there be any action to be taken against anyone, it is for you to suffer for rubbishing their identity. Not me, I won't suffer anything for being truthful about my welfare, your welfare and the welfare of everyone else!'

******

Politicians and civilians are like night and sun. When night falls, the sun seems to have been defeated, but when the sun rises the night can't keep still- it disappears.

******

Everything I wrote is nonsense. It is not because I did not want to write sense. It is because when those whose sense failed to produce sense for all, I decided to communicate sense through nonsense and ultimately produce sense for all.

******

When an empire is collapsing, those who think they are doing it a favour by trying to keeping it standing still shall regret when the empire collapses totally.

******

A President who always demeans the rights and liberties of his people shall always complain of having his authority demeaned.

******

To believe in fear as your savior (liberator) is to live a victim elsewhere.

******

The real war between a politician and an artist is that the former is an unconscious driver of the society, and the latter exposes such a deficiency.

******

A soldier is a civilian. The government of every society cannot claim ownership over them.

******

The government of every society is not a kingdom without its people.

******

A change, if it doesn't come so soon, it needs people to come over it so soon!

******

The only service you can give to a failing nation and corrupt politicians is to download the nation, delete corruption and upload a new nation and politicians.

******

Sometimes people are like tools. Once used, your users dump you and stop being in need of your service.

******

In the political sphere the Bible is always abused as a tool of oppression, and the politicians' best weapon against the people (civilians).

******

If civilians continue to believe in politics as a
religion sacred, the politicians shall remain their gods.

******

I don't see any reason why we should abide by laws that
bind us continuously to oppression.

******

If there is a Minister without portfolio it must also mean
there is a Professor and a Doctor without qualifications!

******

If government takes long to transform a people, the
people will transform the government.

******

Diplomacy is that art of saying 'yes to peace' until you
get a gun.

******

In a society where politicians find no enemy, to demand your rights and liberties is always mistaken as a crime equal to treason. This, if not carefully guarded against and courageously confronted, becomes the oppressor's permanent tool of oppression against a people.

******

War is a right, but to fight always is absurdity.

******

A kingdom build from war knows how to keep peace with others.

******

It is not that the people do not need a President, but they need a President who exercises authority over his Cabinet for the good of the citizens.

******

The people without a leader are butchered elsewhere like criminals.

******

If you can't divide a people, rule them in their divides.

******

Bitter battles define heroes.

******

What makes war long in nature is that in every single war there are many battles.

******

In a world of dictators, the freedom of mankind is a crime.

******

A bitter struggle is in the size of a grievance.

******

The weight of grievance is in the size of the war.

******

The hope to be freed, if it is not followed and accompanied by genuine desires to struggle might be a nightmare of oppression forever.

******

To suppress a revolution whose time has come is to make several struggles in one war.

******

A revolution is an art of change.

******

To deny a revolution in peace is to sign treaties with war.

******

A change that comes so soon is that which has no cause.

******

A minister or politician who shits on the mass, sins against his career.

******

Where freedom of individuals and corporate societies is hard to come by, only change can restructure communities in the ways of justice, only if the individuals and corporate world engages. Do not wait to be engaged. Just engage yourself and urge others to join in bringing change for the better in the landscape of freedom and justice. Do not persecute the freedoms of your neighbor and give the impression that freedom of mankind and justice among individuals is impossible. Such world is what people should say goodbye to! Otherwise you might not have a heritage to pass on to the generations to come.

******

Peace does not mean the absence of war- it means people are reluctant to be in arms.

******

Justice is when your welfare is judged by the state of well-being of your neighbor. Do not look at your neighbor low density suburbs and say all is fine. Look after your neighbor in medium and high density, and improve the peasant in the countryside. Together we can give the world a better look when we took it as each one of us' moral responsibility to transform the destinies of others for the better.

******

Serious wars that consume mankind the worst are decided where guns are not engaged.

******

Only a government with a cabinet of morons and gluttons, rule without the support of the mass.

******

The freedom of individuals- if not shared, connected and networked with the general citizens makes tyrants of those claiming to be freed.

******

In an undemocratic society, people are persecuted for crying for freedom.

******

In the olden times you have heard that the battles are for the bold and strong. But today I say the battles are not for the bold and strong anymore. They are for the weak and bold to fight using borrowed weapons. Battles are meant for the weak to fight while the strong relax in the history that they were once winners (victors)

******

A government that says no to people's grievances invites war, and sins against world peace.

******

A constitution, if it does not give its citizens the right to live freely is just but less than a toilet tissue. It is invalid from the day it was endorsed until the day people revolt against it.

******

A constitution that guarantees its leaders the right to victimise its residents/citizens is a bill for politicians, and the people have the right not to refer to it in the courts of laws.

******

Unless Africa makes efforts to have a name identifiable as hers and restore her identity, nothing can differentiate her from the rest except for the colour of her people.

******

An artist is a non-uniformed soldier. He can continue to defend the government, if the state is not a rebel against him.

******

There's no better colonizer than an oppressor.

******

A lot of yes men at long last make a big no against their own freedom.

******

Do not be signatory to a freedom and peace treaty where you are not allowed to disagree and be convinced.

******

Sometimes to be a rebel is the best way to move a motion and pursue progress.

******

Corruption is a cancer. If not carved out of human flesh today, there is no guarantee that tomorrow it shall heal because the growth would have expanded and spread to the rest of the body.

******

Fear breeds oppression, and those who fear are not free from being oppressed.

******

If patriotism means to be corrupt, to oppress and betray the citizens, I better be a rebel and lead the opposition in what is right!

******

Those who fear have the power to arrest their own liberty, and deny others freedom.

******

Freedom is not like money. People should not bargain for it. It must be guaranteed to everybody, regardless of whether the citizens know about their rights and liberties. Only those who follow this doctrine get reckoned as good or great leaders, and are free from clashing with their people.

******

Wars the world over are founded on differences amongst mankind such as race, skin colour, tribe, religion, creed or *cracy* of demos- these exist in nature. They are found when those who are freed, others were used as ransom to free them, refuses to pay the price to redeem and set free those who were used as ransom.

******

The greatest problem for mankind, as far as freedom is concerned is that everybody needs to be freed, but the majority are not prepared to pay the price to be freed forever.

******

If you no longer want your President to be in power, do not say to him 'Go, Mr. President!' but say 'Come, Mr. President!' To give the President exits is worse than inviting him and his Cabinet to the terraces and then give those who are taking over a bigger audience or mass to rule.

******

I have fought many governments in one book, and why should one government feel like I am a subject of persecution simply because I have used specific names and that particular society to reflect the world in crises?

******

Some rulers are born oppressors but some are oppressors when they become heartbeats of dying or dead empires.

******

When freedom refuses to come in peace, it threatens to come through war.

******

Dangerous rebels do not carry guns around- they carry pens and spell wars from ink.

******

Writers are permanent rebels in every society.

******

A government that is just to its people is free from being accused of being mean with its resources.

******

The world is continuously in wars, and there is no any single moment when mankind was not involved in war- because even in the absence of guns, people do fight with words.

******

The reason why the world is not at peace is that when people need leaders, they get rulers- and when they need rulers, they get persecutors.

******

The time of becoming a rebel is when government declares war against her people.

******

A man who knows his rights and liberties does not see a gun as a threat- but as a friend to his freedom.

******

To get comfort from the nothingness of independence is the courage of fear.

******

Elsewhere, the remaining form of oppression is where people are constantly reminded of independence that never materialized in the lives of the majority.

******

Do not preach freedom of people who are not freed. Preach freedom of people who are freed, and when you preach freedom of the people, know who are freed in that freedom, and help others out of captivity.

******

Diplomacy is the art of withdrawing all the foreign currency from circulation and giving Zimbabweans bond notes- without a single Zimbabwean suspecting that a bond-note is not money.

******

I am always divorced to institutions, political affiliations and religious associations where my liberty and that of the majority others is sacrificed to give unlimited freedom to those who are our oppressers. At first, I thought I was a rebel- but at last, I understand I was a freed man.

******

When power lies with you do not wield it with no sense of posterity in mind because it won't be with you forever.

******

It is pathetic that most governments, especially those in developing societies have become gangsters against their own people. The Presidents and their Cabinets as political servants of the State and have refused to occupy their humble positions as serving servants and be loyal to their masters. Instead, they have become rulers, thieves, robbers and bullies who persecute and murder their masters.

******

The time of becoming a rebel and to go to war is when the ballot box refuses to vote in favor of your choice.

******

If politicians are really servants of the state- then to have politicians escorted by security and leaving the people vulnerable, and at the messy of such security, is not true to the relationship that the politicians are servants and people or citizens are masters.

******

To fight a war in which the very oppressed people you seek to liberate will die more than their oppressors is as good as a well-schemed mass genocide against a people. Such a war should not be approved in the first instance.

******

If you want to change a Government, you must first change the people.

******

A people without a government are subjects of tyrants.

******

Those who are bitter at our differences are not far from venting their own frustrations by becoming dictators themselves.

******

Do not use your freedom to redeem lies- for only but the truth shall set you free.

******

Patriotism is not one sided where the people protect their leaders or rulers without the leaders protecting their people- that one is dictatorship and is oppressive. I have always observed that people, as citizens in their different societies, play their part to service the State but leaders as rulers take their people for granted.

******

More than always, people are the chief enemies of the change they want because if people decide to do away with their Government (politics and politicking) no Government elsewhere can remain a permanent oppressor and impostor against her people.

******

Freedom as an achievement of every society is the transference of power from rulers to the people and leaving the leaders to influence the destiny of a people or of their people.

******

Politics is a virus. It takes justice to cure it.

******

A society with writers is free from rebellions, except when the President and the Cabinet are dictators.

******

Every President elected is a democrat- but it is how much you fear him that makes him a dictator.

******

Do not live in freedom with chains. Leave the chains, and live freely in freedom without chains.

******

Africa is a sample of a society without liberty or freedom.

******

A man who does not appreciate differences is at the risk of becoming a dictator.

******

To fight an oppressor, you must start by fighting the oppressed- because unless you defeat the oppressed, you can never conquer the oppressor.

******

If politicians are servants of the state, then citizens or people are masters of their Presidents and Ministers- and if that be true, then a politician who accounts not to his people and persecutes them for demanding an account he owes them is a rebel himself.

******

Most liberators come like rebels- but it is when people come to their senses and appreciate the need for a change that liberators would then stop being perceived as rebels.

******

Freedom is like a contract. If not renewed on regular basis, it eventually lapses and become oppression.

******

There's no trace of peace and justice that was never redeemed at gun-point. If ever- it was war all the time.

******

A dictator who develops his people is equally a democrat.

******

In most developing societies, corrupt politicians are like a mosquito that sucks from a genitalia- and the reason why they don't go behind bars is that a mosquito that sucks blood from testicles receives the softest slap.

******

A democrat who cannot develop his people equals a dictator and an oppressor.

******

The main reason why we still talk of oppressors and tyrants, even in the 21st Century, is not purely constitutionally or anything to do with our policies. It is because the oppressors and tyrants are people's best friends. And such is a disgusting truth especially when we know for sure that the people are the host and the tyrants and oppressors are only but bugs and ticks- just a squash away.

******

If the politicians are parasites and the people are hosts- then it is true that no politician is bigger than his people.

******

Don't endure to be a sufferer of injustice when your oppressors are enjoying more than abundance. Do not live to enjoy the freedom that has not freed you, and pretend to be at liberty- free yourself and be a lesson to other people to free themselves. Do not postpone your victory- life is too short to be lived in the worst of your citizenship.

******

A lie is the lightest but most dangerous tool or weapon of mass destruction.

******

When we get into a world of freedom, writers stop to be story-tellers. They become historians. They would stop to write in metaphors- instead they would be employed to record the historical achievements of the time. It is when freedom becomes an achievement that no one would be tasked to remind or tell us about our freedoms- we will have to live it, and be a living testimony of freedom we would have achieved for our society. Do not live that freedom on behalf of others and claim that the society is freed- let everyone live their own freedom, and testify that they are freed.

******

The greatest freedom people need is the freedom from poverty, and justice at law.

******

We do not need shells, bombs and guns to destroy the whole world. We only need lies. The heartbreaks, separations and divorces, the strikes and demonstrations, the clashes and rebellions, the hatred and hostilities, the conflicts, violence and wars are all evidence of how destructive are lies.

******

As you fight to liberate yourself do not forget that another serious form of oppression is where the national resources are used as campaigning aids and gimmicks to benefit only individuals who identify themselves with the Party egos.

******

There is no worst and dangerous form of colonization than creating an environment where you will be robbed of the few dollars and cents you would have made, kidnapped or murdered by your fellow countryman.

******

If colonialism and oppression is to be a relic of the past, people in whatever societies ought to stop a habit of associating colonialism with white skins or yellow bones because even a Blackman is a colonizer. If people keep still in these racist mentalities, the society of mankind shall never stop to suffer from plagues of stunted growth and unbecoming development. They should adopt the millennium mindset and address ills of the society, regardless of color and bar codes. I see the society of mankind happily ever, and freely everywhere.

******

If the Government of your day closes down the Textile Industry, then the best form of demonstration is to walk naked in the streets. Do not keep yourself a tenant when Government refuses to give you accommodation- live in the streets and pay no rentals!

******

There are two forces that govern the society of man. One is the force of law and the other is the law of force. Do not be bound in the law of force and pretend that you are in the safe hands of the force of law- because the force of law is a savior and a lord of responsibility but the law of force is an oppressor and a tyrant. Do not be arrested in fears and be a captive- arrest fears and be free.

******

A good leader is not a breeder of factions. He accepts criticism and when ruled by it he is eager to learn and to do what is good.

******

A good leader is ruled by criticism.

******

Colonialism is the evidence of how Powerful States (Whites) or Imperial Forces can be a nuisance if treated with no suspicion and entertained with no brakes.

******

The greatest war each one of us has to fight is the war to conquer and arrest our own fears. Do not hesitate- fear is like a stroke, it doesn't take chances to conquer and arrest you. Release yourself and live freely ever.

******

Our freedom is not stamina of gymnastics and mass displays which goes with stern warnings that 'Do not try it at home!' Practice your freedom and exercise your rights wherever you are and help the world to be free.

******

Slave trade is the chief culprit against the rights and liberties of all species of mankind. It should have not happened in the first instance. I equate it to mass genocide against the developing world. The same way it was abolished, so should be its descendants; slavery, oppression, suppression, repression and all forms of tyranny.

******

Africa is a ransom used to redeem Europe kidnapped in a financial quagmire and to pay off the debts of America (Western World) and to cleanse the curses that befell Australia. In as much as we do not cut off this umbilical cord that connects developing world and the developed world- and develop ourselves, the developing world will never develop forever and ever. And this is amen.

******

The curses that befell Africa are not African. They are foreign in nature, but locally engineered. Not even education is our rescue to break off these curses. This diaspora nemesis and brainwashing syndrome is the latest neo manifestation of slave trade even in the 21st Century.

******

At the height of neo-colonialism in Africa, Africa will be remotely a colony of the Western World.

******

Governments are like books. After they reign they must receive some reviews and feedbacks. A society that keeps a good record of this is a progressive one- and is not afraid of succeeding elsewhere in its lifetime.

******

Power without knowledge is suicide and failure.

******

The end of slave trade, beckoned the colonization of Africa and signaled the beginning of the worst forms of slavery in Africa. Yes slave trade ended, but slavery continued. And by leading the abolishing of slave trade, Britain was not a saint enough neither should her acts be attached to any moral responsibility nor humanitarian ones because Britain had enough reserves and excesses of slaves captured and trapped in America and the diaspora, and had already emerged a powerful beneficiary from this evil than any of her European competitors in the game. Thus by abolishing Slave Trade Britain was being selfish and greedy enough as she wanted to maintain herself a winner, rather than doing this good out of genuine sympathies for slaves.

******

If end of Slave Trade was based on genuine sympathies for slaves and true realization that making subjects of other citizens slaves is inhumane, why did Britain and her folks sustained slavery by resorting to colonization of Africa as an alternative?

******

For not carrying the DNA of Western World, Africa can never be within the provision of Britain's good works of charity- and to have a single moment where we see ourselves as liberated by the Western World is like the pulse of dreams never came true. Africa can only be a beneficiary from Western World's good policies by coincidence rather than by craft of love and true sympathies. This is a true sad reality, without any racist prejudice. If Africa does not take chances to define or redefine herself amongst the world of United States and Big Powers, then the world of Spoon Feeders is over. It is either Africa will rise in immediate context or else she will be recolonized because as I speak, her erstwhile colonizer continues to see her through the lance of prejudice as sea of slaves without jobs- the white man will bring jobs, and the process of re-colonization will begin but without creating economic sustainability for the African mass and the future generations.

******

Liberty without rights is not justice at its best.

******

Through colonialism, European powers transplanted European problems into Africa. It is such problems which when they grew into poverty and diseases, unemployment, industrial closures, individualism and corruption, racism, segregation and discrimination- they became a permanent form of colonialism upon the once colonized societies.

******

To have liberty without rights is a sign of being denied responsibility.

******

Poverty is a weapon in the hands of Mighty States to destroy and victimize Small States.

******

For how long shall we keep waiting for a change? If the change is in you, why are you not speaking it out and make a difference? When the change is in me, I speak it out for development to occur.

******

A people is a ruler of their Rulers. When a Ruler becomes a dictator, he refuses to be ruled by his people- and a Ruler like that is good when thrown out of power.

******

To have a great man like Mugabe, compromising his legacy is a shame upon self and sin against the History of Africa. I have criticized Mugabe, not because I don't subscribe to this religion called African Politics where Mugabe is a god revered, but I have criticized him because for Great Man we hold in high esteem, it is an act of betrayal if we allow him to destroy his own legacy. Mugabe has achieved as a Revolutionary Icon of Africa, and we cannot keep allowing reversal of the gains of his legacy. He should be a gentleman enough, and step down. For a Statesman like him, that alone won't make him a loser- it is not a loss, in fact it will amount to him as a greatest achiever of all times who exited office with the whole world in smiles. We are not saying that his exit should be done in order to send the world smiling because with or without the exit of Mugabe, the world can still smile and frown- but we are saying Mugabe is a point of reference for what is good for Africa, and he should not compromise such a legacy by dying in power. He should have retired much earlier and start to write books about his own struggles and experiences- and the books can be used as reference for this world and future worlds.

******

When we criticize Mugabe, we have absolutely nothing to benefit from it. He has more to benefit or gain from these criticisms- unfortunately his Cabinet is a Circus of bargainers, determined to shut up criticism and good at unleashing anger, frustration, persecution and execution to those who dared criticize Mugabe. It is so pathetic that they don't appreciate that we are doing this in order to protect him- and not destroy his legacy or frustrate his aspiration. We are doing this to keep him in line with the rest of those who have served Africa to their best. If I don't do him this favor when he deserves it through criticism, he will derail and be at odds with the History and Ideals of liberating a progressive African society.

******

When asked if Mugabe was a dictator, I said 'Yes he was a dictator but his dictatorship defined his strength and saved the continent. But a further extension of his dictatorial cable will whip into line, even those who are supposed to whip and toe him into line.' I went on to express my fear and said, 'I fear that at that point in time he might be identified as Napoleon of Africa, but not Benito Mussolini of course- maybe a Hitler of Africa, and a human rights offender.'

******

Corruption is the greatest sanction against developing societies.

******

The Liberation Struggle against the White minority oppressive rule in Zimbabwe and elsewhere across Africa is evidence that Africa was never liberated from slavery and the twin killings through Education or Missionary doctrines. Instead Education and such missionary theologies and mythical doctrines are identified to be chief culprits behind perpetuating mass genocide and oppression.

******

If imperialism is the highest stage of development-then by remaining undeveloped we are not preparing ourselves to counter and defeat imperialism.

******

A war against imperialism is won by achieving justice for your own people.

******

The independence of many developing societies is independence of nations without people. It's practically true-check in your nation if the people are really freed!

******

It is a worst reality to note that before colonization of Africa, Europe was never able to host a major war elsewhere in their history of existence. The two major World Wars of 20th Century AD ever fought by mankind are evidence of how Europe was amass in wealth and cursed by riches looted from Africa. Africa was the funder behind these major wars.

******

No amount of groupings, alliances and weaponry can defend you or us against imperialism or neo-imperialism- justice is the permanent cure against imperialism. Rise above factions and divisions, share and distribute wealth equally amongst your people and be united against the aggressors- and imperialism will never continue to exist.

******

Selfishness, greediness and corruption are true permanent friends of imperialism- where they exist, imperialism is a reality and a menace forever.

******

All societies are independently dependent. No society can live or survive in isolation- a nation borrows from a nation and lends to a nation, so as are continents. We are one in a universe- so is interdependence.

******

Interdependence is the highest stage of independence.

******

Mugabe at his senior age lacked the vigour and practical servitude required for a Statesman to be effective. He was no longer the same energetic, visionary Statesman and pulse of politics we had known back in the earliest days of his reign- he had become more of a theory without practice and enforcement.

******

Do not shut down life, because you once suffered from differences or numerously from persecution and victimization. Struggle until you win the battle against your adversaries and rivalries.

******

To invoke injustice on your people is a self-defeatist policy. If you pursue it, your societies and communities will never rise and ever see the age of their best.

******

The success of every nation is in dispensation of justice. Those who do not dispense justice freely to their people will never stop from falling.

******

If you want to invite war upon yourself and your government, withhold justice from your people.

******

If you can't give justice to your people, give them a flourishing economy- and they will have nothing to do with justice except just a few aspiring to be politicians too.

******

A failing economy is a genuine excuse to start a war. If you want proof on this one, just start destroying your own economy and see a whole people (nation) rising against you.

******

A great Statesman is defined by the welfare of his people.

******

It is not always true that a year is 12-months complete. If a Zimbabwean in Zimbabwe can receive his salary equivalent one month after 3-months or 6-months or once a year- it must also mean that the Zimbabwean Calendar is either 4-months or 6-months long…

******

A Revolution does not start a revolution. It starts as a clamour for reforms, and when not addressed, it becomes open objections, demonstrations and strikes, conflicts and revolts before it eventually gets organized into a protracted struggle.

******

Revolutions are started by those who refuse to cede power to others- and not by those who fight for their turn to get power. It is nonetheless unfortunate that a general tendency is to label rebels or dissidents those who fight for their own turn, share or portion of power and reign.

******

Dictators always think that they can keep a Revolution under lock until they are overthrown by it.

*****

The essence of power is in sharing it. Power is not a one-man achievement- it should be allowed to rotate, and not to remain still in the hands of an individual or individuals, if the society and societies are to be protected from rebellions and war.

*****

I do not support Mugabe- neither do I support Tsvangirai or Donald Trump. I support the people- and I am not afraid of the choice I have made because it is a decision best.

*****

Every politician is a small man. He can only seem to have become a big man when he successfully conquers his people with fear. If you successfully conquer that fear, the politician remains a small man and servant ready to serve his State and prosper his people.

*****

A free people are not prisoners of their freedom. If they can't serve freedom- then they should save, freedom.

******

It is not so much of political problems that make peace to be threatened by war. It is so much of economic problems and social injustices that make war a threat to peace.

******

Test all freedoms, for not all freedoms are all freedoms.

******

War is part of negotiations. Sometimes, if not always- people can never start to take you seriously until and unless you mean danger to those who would be denying you your right to liberty, justice, peace and order.

******

Our struggle to achieve that which we lack always says it is half time to success. Half time is not fulltime- you still have to battle it out for you to become a winner at the end of the match.

******

For a society to be prosperous, people should be taught to work, and politicians should be taught not to steal. Industries are for the people and Jails for the politicians- as a rule of progress.

******

A good politician is a liar.

******

Politicians are good in politics, just like economists are good in economy. If politicians trespass into economy- then what they will do there is not ruling, but ruining the economy. Let politician rule in politics for economists to rule in economy- if a nation is to stand successful and a people prosperous.

******

A poor dictator, if he can't rule you free- he will ruin you free.

******

Empires are built on wisdom, not on education. For example the post-independent Zimbabwe suffered multiple fractures, crises and nemesis up to the point of death under a distinguished academic, scholar and one of the most educated President- none other than his Excellency R.G Mugabe.

******

It appears this world is to be ruled by uncles. After Uncle Sam, it was uncle Bob, and after Uncle Bob, it is most likely that it will be Uncle Trump- and so forth.

******

Every politician is his people's hideout- there is no evil he can commit which his people cannot testify. People are witnesses to everything a politician do.

******

When asked why I seem not to be afraid of the President and his Cabinet, I said 'The state is mine, and I am a master – and the President and his cabinet are servants of the State, and how can a master be afraid of his servants?' ——

******

Sometimes I blame people for allowing themselves to be ruled over and be made subjects or slaves instead of citizens of their society- and be taken for granted by their rulers. If such a relation exists between the government and its people, poverty will never end in developing societies and corruption will continue to be a self-made sanction and a home grown neo-imperialism.

******

Dictatorship does not always relate to system of governance. Sometimes, it is inability to eradicate poverty and improve the livelihood of your people.

******

If this world does not succeed in eradicating corruption, poverty will prosper and diseases will continue to ravage our people- the society shall never be free from wars, and the welfare and lives of our people will continue to be endangered from man-made causes and curses.

******

When being deported to your country becomes a nightmare and a time of seeing yourself as having been sentenced to a long jail term, then something is wrong with your society.

******

When asked if I had the evidence of what I 'claimed' about Mugabe and Government, I responded 'What evidence do I need apart from the mere fact that I was born under Mugabe's rule, grew up reacting to ugly truth, grinded under his carelessness and his abandoned (not followed) domestic policies, suffering from the negligence of his ministers and always made to endure the grueling and harsh experiences under this overrated Statesman? I am not a foreigner- I was born and bred in suffering Zimbabwe. I am not relying on handouts of second hand information- mine is first hand information.'

******

I wanted to spare Mugabe from this bitter criticism, but to spare Mugabe is to breed clowns like him who will prove toxic to the future of a people we seek to establish. Sparing him is like celebrating a dead legacy which will produce wrong people and wrong mindsets that cannot take us forward as progressively as one people and save us and generations to come from continuous bitter wars and struggles. We are not robots that do not think why red, green or yellow- and keep reading stop to one car, even where there are no other cars at the intersection.

******

There are 4 types of people who are extremely difficult to advise; the first one is a woman in love, the second is a man with money, third is a ZANU PF supporter and the fourth one is follower of a prophet.

******

The last moments of Mugabe in power were the worst moments of his reign.

******

Mugabe is part of the African heritage, and I believe by now he should have been in our archives.

******

Man like Nelson Mandela is not only an African heritage, but is also a great founder of a democratic society in Africa. To him, we do give the credit of being "Father Democracy" in Africa.

******

If you are born a Prince and die a Prince, you are a nuisance to the world. You ought also to be a slave and work for others, you ought to be kidnapped and escape, you ought to be also the son of a peasant and get to know how it is like to grow in a poverty stricken family of many children, you ought to suffer it all in order to understand thoroughly who is who, where and how, and improve the situation of everybody everywhere before you can resume your kingship again. Rulers of that nature do not lack- they know, they understand, and are eager to do big for the people, develop the society and conquer poverty, diseases, and wars.

******

The only way we can bring wars to an end is when we move towards a point where those who start wars will have to be put on the forefront of battle force and risk losing their own lives too. If they survive, they will declare ceasefire and go to peace- if they perish on the battlefront, then we are set free as people, and no one shall be a starter of war. We want to eradicate war completely from this world, poverty next and diseases next on list- and how can that be if we only have manuals of war and not peace, manuals of corruption and not of development, manuals of those on death roll and not manuals of life, manuals of what we don't desire to have and not manuals of what we desire to have? Wake up nations, wake up continents, wake up the world- it is now time up and not later to adopt the manuals of life, peace, freedom from exploitation and manipulation, freedom from injustices and corruption, freedom from poverty and diseases, freedom from wars and hunger, freedom from lacking ever and be abused, freedom from lies, graft, craft and all forms of vices, freedom to live freely ever, loving ever, happy ever, growing ever, developing ever and becoming abundant in saving humanity and the universe.

******

I have known Mugabe from a close range. He is a great philosopher, an encyclopedia of encyclopedias, a walking dictionary and a moving strong arsenal but certainly not a President par-excellent!

******

A writer is a politician.

******

Africa is not blackout of ideas. She is a blackout of implementation.

******

The state is my homeland, but I am an independent candidate.

******

Building a nation is not billing a nation. Building a more modern society involves vision about a nation where your children and Bolt Cutter's children can live happily, unconstrained by the shackles of obsolete thinking, yet grounded in the traditions and culture of your society. Zimbabweans ought to do this, Africans follow suit and the world outside is freed from blame.

******

Dahomey was a modern state in Ancient times.

******

Africa today is a modern society in her diseased lot. I am not very sure if a blood transfusion will work for her, but certainly she needs capital or financial injections and start to receive serious medication in her intensive care unit once we successfully do away with the gluttons and parasites sucking and draining blood off her dying economies.

******

Names like Mugabe cannot be written once in a book and you say the book is complete. It has got to be written many times for the book to make sense. That man is indeed great!

******

Discovering politicians or a politician like Mugabe takes an apolitical mind. Don't be a racist, don't be partisan or a factionalist!

******

Democracy starts the day you are fooled when you want to be full.

******

Democracy is the weakest point of politics.

******

At the highest stage of Democracy, people will clamour for dictatorship.

******

The furthest you can reach with Democracy is dictatorship.

******

Politics is politic of tricks.

******

If you want to be a President without campaigning for the post, be a wife of the President.

******

Man like Emmerson Dambudzo Mnangagwa of Zimbabwe and the likes are favourable species of mankind unfortunate indeed to be victims of bad publicity. I do not seem to see how he is a devil himself except that those unfamiliar with Lacoste antics make him a devil!

******

We believe that ZANU PF might have shifted goal-posts for a country dedicated or committed to score after independence, but I do not believe that some individuals within the party are not also free from blame. People are free to name-calling but a few selected also deserve name-praising.

******

What made Zimbabweans not prosper as a nation is not that they are stupid or disunited. It is that they are united in cowardice.

******

Considering that Zimbabwe is geographically small, it is very naïve and stupid of her authorities and or disturbing to anyone to imagine why Zimbabwe is not prospering her people when she is just but abundantly a rich province of South Africa or China?

******

In this world if we scream in the voice of Bob, we will be made youth and tools to lead operation forced ejaculation and if we scream in the voice of citizens to be freed we will be the people on the cursed lot and ultimate victims to be forced ejaculation ourselves.

******

With ZANU PF, Zimbabweans have been reduced to "yes man".

******

Mugabe should not be wholly condemned. As a founding father of African politics and godfather of Zimbabwean politics, he has had health brains but sick action.

******

The Zimbabweans are too educated for the Zimbabwean crises.

******

Education is a political misfit.

******

To eliminate Mnangagwa from Zanu PF party is the greatest blunder, Zanu PF will regret ever. The man is a damn shit schemer of the art of intelligence in all camps. I repeat, he is a shrewd schemer and a reliable gun and or muscle. Without him, Zanu PF is on the embers of extinction!

******

When it comes to saving the Party Zanu PF, Mnangagwa was the only man I have seen so far selflessly committed to do whatever possible to keep the party surviving.

******

I know Jonathan Moyo. He is a set of poorly utilized knowledge and abused intelligence. His is only but a daring mind, guided by tribal constitution rather than common good for the nation.

******

Jonathan is the energy behind Grace. The whole move, although it is intended to eliminate Mnangagwa and loyals, Zanu PF will surely wake up to see even Grace and those running as anti-Lacoste also doomed in a political drain.

******

The people of Zimbabwe shall remain with no option except to vote for Opposition not because they like the opposition, but because the Ruling Party is a ruining party!

******

Mugabe was once a gentleman.

******

Having exhausted his strength and genius in power, it is now more apparent than claim that Mugabe is less than the history that elevated him to power.

******

What keeps ZANU PF surviving is a selfish agenda of those so few benefiting from its existence, not that the Party has done so much good than harm to its people.

******

So what Zimbabweans regarded as a constitution was rather a toilet tissue and Zimbabweans were run using raw ideas straight from the Head of the politiburo? It is not only shameful but also pathetic!

Printed in the United States
By Bookmasters